# Bridge and Tunnel

# Bridge and Tunnel

Poems by John Hennessy

Turning Point

*[signature: John J Hennessy]*

For Arthur,

With admiration—from

one who wishes to play

Old John Falstaff—

*John*

Published by Turning Point
P.O. Box 541106
Cincinnati, OH 45254-1106

Typeset in Garamond by WordTech Communications LLC, Cincinnati, OH

ISBN: 9781933456553
LCCN: 2006940551

Poetry Editor: Kevin Walzer
Business Editor: Lori Jareo

Cover artwork and design: Mira Bartok

Visit us on the web at www.turningpointbooks.com

# Acknowledgements

5AM: "My House and the House Next Door"

Fulcrum: "Driving the Causeway," "The Cannibals Come to Seminary Ave.," "Two Ogres," "Perpetuum Carmen," "Pictures with Krishna," "In the Kills" (part IV), "The Polish Question," "Why Not Dig Up the Dog?" "Winter Garden," "Guardian Angels," and "My Date with Satan"

The Greensboro Review: "Dialing While Intoxicated" and "Dreaming of Feet"

Harvard Review: "Quiet Only When He Ate" (as "Ariadne on Naxos") and "How the Dog-Star Got His Name"

Jacket: "New Corinthian: Letter to Paul"

LIT: "My Mother Explains" and "Shaved Head"

The Massachusetts Review: "My Father Explains"

New Letters: "Nixon's Last Days, Seminary Ave."

The New Republic: "Signing the Kills"

Notre Dame Review: "My Son's Lost Languages," "Vengeance," and "Calling"

Ontario Review: "Hyon Gok Sunim," "Love Along the Rahway River," "My Father's House," "In the Kills" (parts I-III)

Poetry Northwest: "Pan in Arkansas"

Press: "Cusp"

Rattapallax: "Newark Underground" (as "Orpheus in Newark")

The Sewanee Review: "The Raft of the Medusa," "Urban and His Daughter," "Irish Washerwomen in the New World," "Dr. Swann," and "Missing Carnival"

Smartish Pace: "Drift" (as "Charon and Persephone")

Third Coast: "Free Union"

Washington Square: "Dog-Star Freddy"

Willow Springs: "Mike Devlin" and "Nicholas, Flying"

The Yale Review: "Bachelorhood"

"My Father Explains" was reprinted on Poetry Daily.
"Why Not Dig Up the Dog?" was reprinted in Best New Poets, 2005.
"Signing the Kills" was reprinted on Verse Daily.

Thank you to Mira Bartok for her artwork on the cover.

for Sabina

It is not the spiritual which is first
but the physical, and then the spiritual.
　　　　　—Paul, *1 Corinthians*, 15: 46.


Venus was ready to desert her Cyprus,
to leave her cities and her plains. "And yet,"
she said, "these sites are dear to me, these towns—
what crime is theirs? What evil have they done?"
　　　　　—Ovid, *Metamorphoses*, x.
　　　　　(translation, Allen Mandelbaum)

# Contents

I

Signing the Kills ........................................... 15
Irish Washerwomen in the New World .................... 16
Dog-Star Freddy ........................................... 19
Mike Devlin ................................................ 21
Pictures with Krishna ..................................... 22
The Cannibals Come to Seminary Ave. ................... 24
Drift ....................................................... 25
Nixon's Last Days, Seminary Ave. ....................... 26
Dr. Swann ................................................. 27
Guardian Angels ........................................... 28
My Father Explains ........................................ 29
My Mother Explains ....................................... 30
Love Along the Rahway River ............................. 31
Dialing While Intoxicated ................................. 33
Drinking with My Sisters ................................. 34
Cusp ....................................................... 35
Quiet Only When He Ate .................................. 37
Driving the Causeway ..................................... 39
Missing Carnival .......................................... 40
My Date with Satan ....................................... 42
Shaved Head ............................................... 43
Pan in Arkansas ........................................... 45
My House and the House Next Door ...................... 46
Bachelorhood .............................................. 47

II

In the Kills ................................................ 51

# III

New Corinthian: Letter to Paul ................................................... 57

Newark Underworld ................................................................ 58

Dreaming of Feet ................................................................... 60

Winter Garden ...................................................................... 62

The Polish Question ............................................................... 63

The Raft of the Medusa .......................................................... 64

Perpetuum Carmen ................................................................ 67

Urban and His Daughter ......................................................... 68

Vengeance ............................................................................ 70

How the Dog-Star Got His Name .............................................. 71

Free Union ........................................................................... 73

Nicholas, Flying .................................................................... 75

Why Not Dig Up the Dog? ...................................................... 76

My Father's House ................................................................. 77

Two Ogres ........................................................................... 79

Hyon Gok Sunim ................................................................... 80

My Son's Lost Languages ......................................................... 83

Calling ................................................................................ 84

I

# Signing the Kills

That might have been me, the boy you saw
walking below the smokestacks. All night
he crossed the bridges between boroughs,
hitch-hiked rides beneath the rivers.
He stood spread-eagle in the silver webbing
on a dare that came across the airwaves
of his own voice, climbed Hail Mary
up the ladder of enormous cylinders,
fuel tanks and water towers, sprayed
the several syllables of invented names,
tagged overpasses and the underbellies
of train trestles. He walked until it seemed
his voice could mimic even the sound
of shoes slipping on roadside gravel,
the belt rubbing skin on his hips, the straps
of his singlet, the chain clinking against
the Saint Christopher he still believed in.
He baited pigeons and seagulls to play
Saint Francis and he would have tagged them
too, if they'd come. He walked until morning
smoke clouded the stars above the Kills
and doused the distant city's lights.
He tossed the rattling empty spray-can
and walked until he couldn't be distracted.
He walked until that voice was finally quiet.
He walked until those slow clouds started
to billow like offerings at matins and he
was emissary of a generous silence.

# Irish Washerwomen in the New World

Mary Glover, d. 1688, Boston
Margaret Dolan, d. 1980, Brooklyn

> She entertained me with nothing but Irish...However,
> against her will I prayed with her, which if it were
> a fault, it was in my excess of pity.
> > Cotton Mather, *Memorable Providences*

Take Great-grandmother Dolan, with her pocket full
of husbands and several spare names, her salt-spit
and snakebite, poker-face, terrier bitch, Donegal
wit, dog-track bag and four-pronged walking stick,

spin her in a silver capsule or calendar-flap,
time-line back three hundred years, keep her up
in Boston where she first jumped ship (the trap
she set her older sister, a girl whose luck

and nerve gave out when they saw her to the docks),
and I'll give you Mary Glover, Cotton Mather's
confounding hag. It took just a poorly-darned sock
or bit of missing linen, a few saw-toothed

taunts levied at the master's brats (that spray
of wet fricatives doused Goodwin's sallow brow),
the discovery of poppets stuffed with hay
and goat-hair planted in her beams, and slow

justice did a slower fox-trot, clopped Mary off
in a wooden-wheeled gallows cart. A wonder we
weren't as clever, my cousins and I, as that self-
possessed posse—Our Lady of Dun Laoghaire

was spared the Catskills act: the pains that flew
like lightning from limb to limb, blindness that came
and went, traded for speech or hearing, and new
gymnastics, which might make them one minute seem

to be tied neck and heel, skin so tightly stretched
their bellies should split, the next shoulders collapsed,
necks spent, heads twisted half-way around. They twitched
their hips to silent music and finger-snapped,

yodeled or yapped wide enough to snap their jaws
out of joint. Soon the neighbors exhumed her husband's
constant complaint: the woman perverts God's law,
throws top to bottom, and there's not a bloody island

so remote she couldn't track me with her witchcraft
and slip the nails beneath me as I slept.
Grandfather said as much, but his mates laughed
as they were meant to—until our Margaret left,

on to the next while he was still alive,
laid up in hospital with a gangrenous eye
and ice-pick wounds dripping his kidneys dry.
A barman's harvest, she said, and when he died

she skipped the wake and funeral. We did the same
more than four decades later, when the half-dozen
cancers that worked her bones and organs came
to common purpose in her colon. Our puns

and inversions—her conscience didn't sit well,
and appetite caught up with her in the end—
helped keep us this side of Brooklyn, burial
that. We spilled lilies, caps of whisky, pretended

to see her—because witches float. But I've always
secretly wished I'd met the girl beneath,
what burned low and mean, the kerosene base
that fueled the shriveled spit-fire. It's no wreath

of burning cypress, but I'll think of her
sometimes when grubbing celestial favors, ask
that she be minded; even Cotton Mather
stretched his hems, knelt in the flow of heaven's flask

puddling around her feet, when Goody's Latin
Pater Noster got mixed with an Irish blessing.
I see them in relief, Mather's pointed hat, two women
stretching the cord, backlit at sunset, dangling.

# Dog-Star Freddy

He hated anything that flew, he said,
stuffed hooks in chunks of Sunbeam bread and went
pigeon-fishing, hauled scores off leaf-plugged gutters
and out from under eaves on nylon thread,
swung and beat them overhead, the Roman soldier,
new David, bastard of both testaments.

He poisoned sparrows with washroom bleach,
gas in the bird bath, hung them by their feet
from swings at Shotwell Park. Pale little nestlings
hovered like stunned hummingbirds, upside-down.
We stuck to basketball or slammed stickball
off the apartment building wall, crowned the king

of the jungle-gym with stitches, skipped the swings
until he copped a wrist-rocket, cocked at crows.
He plunked them off power-lines and streetlights
with marbles, gravel stolen from building sites,
plucked them before they died, stuck feathers in
his puca-shells, played Vietcong scalps Navajo.

Mid-summer and the whole neighborhood reeked:
sun-burned dumpsters, rat sunk in hallway walls,
drunken vets stumbled singing out of Pete's,
incontinently sprinkled streets,
Merck chemical plant's fuel tank leaked, and all
those rotting birds. Dog-Star inspired, that freak

in stinking feathers took prisoners to his basement
bunker—the smell of lichen, slugs, and newsprint,
and cool, at least. His ambush spread, we all went,
boys, girls, anything with eyes and orifice;
even the youngest made good audience.
Me, I skimmed his porno-stash, watched when asked,

scared, not uninterested, learned words for what
our parents did, studied and waited when he bent
and said, it looks just like a starfish, slot
for human pinball, blazing Aztec sun,
a burning basketball, it's where I vent
the souls of all the birds I catch, it's one

odd nest: sick, yes, but subject to his muse.

# Mike Devlin

The dairy light, he called it, in any weather
when he delivered—fog eddies from Arthur Kill,
sun half an hour high over Merck, the morning
divided by smokestack. Temper's teacup, a man's
no more than a punter's error, he liked to say.
He hummed "Ave Maria" through the baritone
kazoo of tracheotomy, circus shadow
of his church choir tenor; for kids, he buzzed
the Yankee Doodle like electric razor
or flexed his arm and blackened ship tattoos
dropped anchor under a war wound's purple chop.

After the dairy cut his route, he became our oldest
paper-boy. Sack slung around his shoulder
and cradled like a headless cello, we saw him
more often, his walk an economic waltz.
Warm afternoons, he propped a shoe-shine box
beneath the awnings of Truppa's deli, bullied tips
from all his customers. He slipped his gauze,
pulled the patch off his blow-hole, neck-smoked
a hot-boxed Camel to win the hardest cases.

The night Mike died, men emptied out of Pete's:
Knights, Vets, Legionnaires, Sons of Italy. They parked
a phonograph on the fire-escape and played
his seventy-eights. Crackling Irish tenors
rose along rusted, ivy-covered slats, zigzag
ladder and window grills, to sing us to sleep.
Later bottles dropped, a pipe burst, the record player
smashed in the alley. Beat-cops broke it up
before morning twilight, his old delivery hour.

# Pictures with Krishna

That's Krishna Jain the night I met him
in the basement backstage at the old Palladium,
that shimmer of pink and blue the plate-glass
storefront of Disco Donuts, the last
of us brown-skinned boys leaning in, all lip
and cheekbone, startled attitude. Hadn't it
been him the week before at the Cramps
hoisting me out of the shallows by the amps?
I took his name and picture, began to look
for him at CB's, Dojo, and St. Mark's Books—
that's him dancing at Max's Kansas City—
it seemed a friendly sort of destiny.

Here we are taking the train back to Jersey—
the odd, gray beauty of the refineries,
like gentle creatures of the Pleistocene
balancing fiery crowns and bowing—
and for a year or so I saw him everywhere,
at the Slits in Asbury, the Clash on the pier,
in Famous Ray's, Bleecker Bob's, and Phoebe's;
once at a house party on Avenue B
we both passed out behind the couch—all night
I dreamed of zebras and velveteen, some sight
more frightening than the hooks and fishing line
I'd threaded from ear to nose and back again.

There were others I knew like him, more or less
by sight, but none were so ubiquitous,
none quite the bag-man, mayor, and billboard star,
set-dresser come to move the furniture
or paint a window through that secret teenaged life.
It was like watching palms sprout through ice—
there, in our keffiyeh scarves and army boots,
under Gothic arches, turning leaves, ivy shoots—

imagine—seeing Krishna on campus that first
September: some unarticulated hunch confirmed,
an astrological inevitability;
brother-in-law, best friend, what would he be?

The heavens disappointed, of course; these slides
have limned that friendship's limits. My hunches lied,
and, as you say, they may have more to do
with thrashing through Narcissus' pool
than following a path already traced
along the milestones of the Milky Way.
But that hardly proves all friendships float
the shadows of silvered tributaries; although
I suppose that here he *does* look a bit like me,
just taller, darker, thinner, flat-top buzzie
more severe, his Spartacus Youth shirt redder—
I might have liked his sister if I'd met her.

# The Cannibals Come to Seminary Ave.

They came to us along the bus route
in dug-out canoes, tied up at the banks
near Shotwell Park. Our back-court hustlers

checked them for game. Curtis played ringer
at a dollar a bucket, picked up his uncle,
Indian Sim (still crazy from Nam,

tomahawk dunk), in the five-dollar draft.
Five, ten, twenty, then fifty, double
or nothing—those lard-greased butchers

in toxic gym-shorts, fluorescent Pumas,
made minced meat of the locals. Strung
and bled from backboards, skinned in strips,

the muscle and marbled fat of thighs
and calves cut clean away by flint-
tipped tools with the ancestors' grip—

at day's end it was hard to accept
these racks of bone were our quickest men.
They salted some and hung them to dry,

made offerings to their three-part God
through salty yawns, then cribbed by Curtis
at Riverside Arms, claiming they liked

his view of the river, its chemical greens
and floating fish, and so much salvage
potential in rusting auto-parts.

# Drift

After leaving home and school
and Seminary Avenue, I float
my pallet down the Rahway River, escort
to stately grim Persephone,
twenty-five and she's just got braces,
pock-scars covered with foundation,
magenta pony-tail, black-framed glasses,
jogging bra, skull tattoo, pencil skirt and lace-up boots,
and creeping from a leather satchel
her soiled memoir notes.

We drift past Merck and Exxon,
a single gleaming green
our Northern Lights, time
a broken bird-wing, spleen
the steam that drives us on.
I show her I've saved the dime
struck with her startled profile
and plunge the rubber gag-pole
I use for navigation.
It seems we'll never reach our destination.

Sure, I've learned a tricky back-rub,
shiatsu and aikido, while she
waves hands like clouds, brings tai-chi
and yoga. But honestly, we spend our time
just camping at the bar, the clothesline
strings a canopy, plastic palms drop
cigar stubs like coconuts, mulch spills
from rubber tubs, and overhead
our shadows circle like lazy seagulls
while we trade tales from childhood.

# Nixon's Last Days, Seminary Ave.

Here's no-throw Santiago doing Felix Millan,
full crouch, high choke, no English yet
but the son-of-a-bitch can hit, and it's my ball,
two reasons to keep it in the playground. But
before I can crank my leg for a Juan Marichal
bucket-drop, Radio Mario rides up yelling:
No shit, the president's quit, chanting in time
to grating clicks of his rusted ten-speed, fuzz
buzzing the box strapped to his wrist. Just pitch,
the shortstop shouts. The kick, release, red stitch
of baseball seams whirring in a curve across
the plate cut from a pizza-box, and I'm
sick even before I see it: bat slash, line-drive,
and the messenger laid out under yellow sky.

# Dr. Swann

The gurneys skirr across the room like unmoored
lily pads. Shoulders stooped, neck crooked
to better see beneath the ruptured skin, he snips,
cuts, saws, picks flattened slugs from ribs and liver,
sews cover over palpitating heart, lungs
stripped clean of shot. Blood bags hang and drip,
deltas within the draining deltas he's learned
his practice down, returned from Mekong to canals
and bridges quilting Newark, the skirmishes
along its borders, Arthur Kill to Sandy Hook;
he reminds himself that surgery is blind.
Mornings he backs across the Oranges
by commuter rail, his wake an oil slick,
while shades revive and cross before him, screened
by light reflecting off the barges, thick as smoke.
Those left behind still haunt him, but no more
than some who live, their scars his signature.

# Guardian Angels

Curtis chugged his cup of icicle-drip,
tipped his afro back, dangling pick
as big as a rake, struck pink below
the distillery billboard's martini
glow, red glasses and pimento stones.

He said we were practicing to be
subway angels, bus route marines.
We'd tour the neighborhood bars
and bodegas, take cover under the awnings
of Truppa's deli, Sons of Italy flags.

In the alley behind Reveler's Theater
someone had dumped photos of naked men—
headless white torsos, glistening pricks
and rumps—which burned bunting blue
when we lit them, then sizzled into ash.

The bitter wind strapped hustlers home,
dust-storms tilted around Shotwell Park
and two winos rolled, basement curtains
in Riverside Arms closed. We huddled close
to his mother's lighter, kept cold vigil.

# My Father Explains

Unleashed into the nocturnal world he drew
came a fedoraed tough, slinking like Spade
or Marlowe through streets of murky damp, a mob
of thugs he outwitted with muscular
cunning. He slipped in and out of quais
and alleys until he found his dame, his match,
a woman with an hour-glass wit, come-backs
and kisses like paper cuts. Their embedded

embrace produced a whole series of clues
and red herrings: straight shot of rye, cocktail
clink, green felt field receding under games
of poker and nine-ball, dominant black-jack
strike, a brown-eyed whack, crow-bar damage,
looping, labyrinthine strings of jail cells,
cathouse chambers, and rented rooms, closing on
the howl and bloodbath of birth, a smoking gun.

When he was done I felt pretty good about myself.
With thousands, millions, of questing gumshoes,
each month a sleuthing moll, I'd come from the single
canny pair. And there was something sweepingly
democratic about this fortune, a spike of light
in that tumbler of noir darkness: we all arrived
this way—Protean mystery and darkling solution
in one, all of us survivors of the underworld.

# My Mother Explains

A true Catholic, untroubled by Roman exception,
now that's my mother, the coffee-klatsch cantor,
R-dropping, throat-singing, muezzin of Pat's Diner.
Apprehension begins when prayer stretches thin,
a kite cut from its string, tail of net-stockings
in tortured spin—she sees God in everything.

Her door-guard's a mezuzah darkened by swatches
of insect blood, a welcomed casualty
from warmer weather. She hijacks time away
from Tarot cards and tea leaves, translates quickly
the secrets spread on matzoh crackers. The Church's
high mysteries can't conjure her holy days

or explain the snake-dances she coils and springs
on simple votive candles. She's wired her chakras,
sent sweat-lodges thrumming Bear through Coyote,
uncovered my mission to hunt the deer of pain.
Evil eye, Scorpio moon—now that's some armor,
she says. I prayed for you. You're prayed for, not lucky.

# Love Along the Rahway River

Ball: Nemesis, flat-chested, tow-headed Pole,
daughter of vodka drunks, distillery jocks
who gummed an English all toothless glottal stops
and dry, bread-crust gutturals, found me behind
the Hamilton Street laundry, up to my hips
in the river hunting carp and crayfish

with bacon on a string, advice I'd read
in Twain or Ranger Rick, and useless among
those rusted shopping carts. She said she had
something worth seeing, led me along the bank,
a yellow path we had to crouch to follow
through forsythia scrub. Behind a fort

she'd cobbled from rotting wooden crates,
Ball lay back over leaves and fallen blossoms,
orange silt stranded by floodwaters swilling
past Merck's. In tones as flat as those of men
carrying couches down crowded stairwells,
Ball led me through the act of love, stopping

only to offer an expert gob for lubricant.
I wish I had hummingbirds hidden in
my hat, a Jack of hearts stuffed up my sleeve,
some way to deliver the pleasure that I felt,
but really, what is there to compare it to?
And anyway, that pleasure's been gutted

by memory of the pain which soon replaced it.
We must have been too vigorous, because Ball
began to bleed. She snatched up that swatch
of Saint Mary's plaid, hit me hard in the face.
Bright yellow flash: running civilians in
the war before supper, reluctant bucket-boy

for the Thriller in Manila, Chiller Monster
Cinema's disembodied hand. Both eyes tingled
before reptilian swelling, nose crushed, already
setting in permanent southeastern slant. The smear
on Ball's skinny pink thigh seemed nothing in
comparison, but I learned quickly to call it even.

# Dialing While Intoxicated

Even this late I'm clever as cold coffee
and whisky. Scavenged that desperate pouch
of black shag I should've chucked ages ago,
ashes over-spilling the bread plate, butts
floating in backwash. Cup rings roam
the tabletop, the phone pad, half-stamp
my game of solo hangman. All of the E's
in "every ounce of everclear" busted
my bank long before tonight. But I dial on,
the kite and key of electric currency,
that flash of red, first frost in the maple trees:

in Amsterdam, look who's coming down the canal,
bicycle tires turning, up over the flock of bridges,
hump-backs bent and feeding, and round the crocus
and hemlock circle at Weteringschans. Who knows
which ex- is on the line? Then pub doors open
down Dorset Street, lights go off over Liffey murk,
the kitchen receiver sounds its dull double-bleat.
My sister, single now, searches for the phone.
And in Dunedin, the next day's already broken,
wobbled its way up summer twilight on sea legs,
half a year ahead. I could lick and tuck
one last roll-up, even call there collect.

# Drinking with My Sisters

*M., P., K., & L.G.*

No fun to play Quarters with them, we fought
to lose. And Phil Rizzuto's Holy Cow—
forget home runs, enthusiasm crippled us
by seventh-inning stretch. The movies made

a game of it—we'd wait until the train
set off the inlet horns and trestle bells
to crack the fire-door—and hope our stash
was there. We loved the dollar double features

from Hong Kong, or *Cooley High* and *Cornbread*.
*Eraserhead* at midnight was twilight zone
return to our first home, the rooming house
that smelled of cats and onions; more Dionysian

was *Rocky Horror*—we sniped the kick-line with toast
and rice, and pitched our empty pints. Some nights
we drank Scheherazade, Exquisite Corpse,
and spun adventures for Great Aunt Vita, who looked

like Sammy Davis in Frank Sinatra's wig,
Clark Kent to Superman in Drag. The tallest tale
we told was true: the time we caught our father
creeping downstairs, his shoes in hand, car parked

a block away—when we were coming in, he
was sneaking out. Divorce court, aphrodisiac
to Mom and Dad. And later someone said,
*I'm having an affair with my wife*; we laughed

a long time, drank rounds of five and didn't care
who saw us on the stoop, radio running down
the battery of our car on blocks all night,
and even after the trains and buses ran.

# Cusp

No matter which of his many women
he happens to be with, when the leaves
begin to sink their hooks into the sky
and somewhere over Australia the sun
enters the Ram and clips the cusp of the Fish,
my father calls to talk about the day I was born.

There was a snowstorm before I was born,
which came as some surprise. The old woman
who lived upstairs came down with some redfish
she stuffed with parsley and garlic, baked in grape leaves.
She liked to feed my parents, treated them like son
and daughter. She was the first to notice the sky.

Just a few clouds to start, then the whole sky
flushed white and the afternoon looked stillborn.
It made Dad nervous. You're sure to have a son,
and he'll be born today, said the woman.
She pushed away her plate and sucked a grape leaf,
still savoring the last bits of fish.

The woman, her auguries and her fish,
the first day of spring and a snow-filled sky,
my father already planning to leave
Brooklyn but waiting for me to be born—
maybe he tells the story for the woman
whose bed he's sharing, and not for his son.

It's not easy being such a man's son.
I swim in two directions, like the Fish
I was born under. My father and his women.
Just read the signs suspended from the sky,
I want to tell them. Vernal snow is borne
across Bay Ridge by the force that makes him leave.

I envy that ability to leave.
I'm always coming back. I'd shove the sun
behind the snow on the street where I was born,
I'd breathe the bus exhaust, wet brick, and fish,
I'd convince myself I loved Brooklyn's sooty sky—
and I'd enjoy doing it—for a woman.

You learn from me, Dad says. Leaving a woman
is easy. You're young—your sun heats only half the sky.
When you were born, I was just learning to fish.

# Quiet Only When He Ate

He'd taken Ariadne with him, yet
he showed no pity: on that shore he left
the faithful girl.
      *Metamorphoses*, viii.


Even before he slid out already standing,
His hairless legs more foal than calf—the human
Knees, splayed toes, father's flanks—I saw my brother
Reflected in the bulls-eye mirror, whip-scars
Streaking his shoulders, forehead fading below
His upright ears, face covered with mottled hanks
Of auburn hair, full, bow-shaped lips a joke,
Bulging teeth, tongue rolling uncontrollably.
The sight did not prepare me for the sound
Of him, though: savage bellows giving way
To an obscenity of vicious braying,
A copper wire scratching harp strings.
I saw what frustrated him, what drove
His rage, was that he'd never learn to speak,
That noise was both his fury's source and issue,
His appetites transformed to sound, and it
Provoked as much pity in me as violence
In him, hunger for human flesh just one
More way to express his hatred for himself—
And he was quiet only when he ate.
I swore he wouldn't live. It was a sort
Of love, I guess. Call that love, yes, and this
Unkindness, maybe, but not abandonment.
Some women might prefer a husband's debt,
But I choose stricter solitude, a zodiac
Of my own imaginings, new alphabet,
And even the dumbest stone on Naxos sings
What every vine produces. The greenest wine
Here satisfies. I'll take a skin to hike

The rocks and beaches, spill a bit for my partner
In drink, my closer twin. He's fond of me,
More brotherly than even the human parts
Of that animal. Of both of them, I mean.

# Driving the Causeway

High tide and salt grass hid the causeway, road
sinking instead of rising then. Don't think
this dharmic figure, vatic drivel, the slowed
but luminous path, eight-fold horizon. Shrink

the sky until it's all black-hole and nothing flies,
until it fits inside a shoreman's fist—
at least a thousand things to do, the lie's
the limit, with that still-contracting brick—

and there you have it, the causeway's first effect.
How far from brake to rest; I couldn't move,
I couldn't even start to trace the wreck
from path's beginning to drawbridge end, improve

the honeymoon from gravedigger's bed—cold, wet,
a place that death approaches, but hasn't been
to yet. I'd paint it, if I could, and let
the picture of a crashing car stand in.

## Missing Carnival

*O Venlo, Venlo, stedje van pleseer*. This time
her body made him think of countryside,
some figure from his childhood, sun on scythe,
wind blowing shadows across the shining barley,

the milk-pail dented from use, the smell of leaf-mulch
and leather in the tack room. Soon she'd take bus
and ferry from London to Belfast, but first
the fire in her bed-sit. Her fingers traveled too,

down the raised purple scars along his vertebrae,
the flannel sheets between her thighs, his hair
trailing along her abdomen, the quill
of a feather poking through seams of the comforter,

the comforter itself. Those scars—he'd lied
to her, his time in Nicaragua, thugs cut
him coming from the fields. The bloodier fight
was with his brother, slicing tines of a pitchfork

plucked up along the flooded Maas. Everything
reduced to trinket and anecdote, the beer
and facepaint of carnival, street-dance and tuba,
beyond the muddy English roundabouts, the brown

and white waves, yellow lamps along Dutch highways,
his work at the union office pinned beneath
a glass globe paperweight—shaken
it showered silver snow over the wide

straw hat, red and green plow, the slouching body,
a campesino from days before Somoza fell.
He wondered if she were any better, smuggling
French social theory into Ulster, encounter

groups in the rec-centers of tower-block basements.
She'd just gotten the news: her last lover died
in a fire along the side of the highway, body
broken in seven places, silver chrome,

pearl and gold gas tank scorched, his bike crumpled
beneath the husk of an overturned van.
There wasn't much to talk about. Afterwards she lay
with her back to him and he sang her carnival songs

in a language she didn't speak, *O Venlo, stedje van
pleseer*. He thought of himself as the sun, kissing
her neck at the hairline, turning grey cobblestones
of the town-square silver, marshaling parades.

## My Date with Satan

He brings a bouquet of white tulips,
red-ribboned box with a dress from Prada—
blue sequined halter, tapered train like a mermaid—
is my butt too big? How about my hips?
My ankles are touching, the fit constricts,
I'm breathless, crushed, re-constructed, but he
pats me with his silver, silk-gloved palm,
tells me not to worry—I'm such a tight package—
practically bursting—we kiss in the taxi.

Salome at Lincoln Center—my date's magnificent
in the chandeliered entry, taking his hat off
and stooping—we hold hands to our seats.
He squeezes my thigh when Salome dances,
tugs loose his bow-tie when she squats
on the Baptist and uses his head obscenely,
fist of dark hair held to her crotch. He sings
along under his breath in less
than perfect German, clipping every note.

The car whisks us to the Brooklyn Bridge
and we're laughing, pouring wine in the river,
climbing the scaffolding—my size twelve
satin slippers sail off in the current. The way
back to Jersey, we crash the distillery,
skinny dip in vats of gin and whisky, towel dry
beneath the billboard's clinking pink glasses. But
he drops me off a perfect gentleman, just quick
toothy kisses, pricks appetite I'll tend to myself.

# Shaved Head

Forget contingencies from weather and wind,
my Helen's head was shaved, the shortest bit
of stubble growing in. With darkened arching
black eye-brows, Betty-Blue mouth penciled red,

jet patent-leather trench and high-heeled boots,
she seemed more mannequin for Fashion Ave.'s
penitent spread than enemy to brass
at Camp Lejeune. Simply and grudgingly put,

her talk was action. Invincible in Bell-
Atlantic block and tack, she converted non-coms
and saved CO's, harped flint and skinned the chair
of military courts through well-pitched cheek,

prompt dispatch from the War Resister's League.
She looked good even on a bicycle, hemming left
through traffic on Fourteenth Street, locking up
on Lafayette or Grand. She doused for me

to celebrate—marched right through human waste
and Bowery puddles, stretched her legs over the last
old-fashioned hobos up to East Second Street.
Those ancient days, our vestibule was manned

by crack-dealing Stan, a concierge of wit
and improv, half his face scored by orange scars
from hydrofluoric burns. He kept the place safe.
But I had gone, cleared out behind a gang

of kids from Bronxville high on catnip wins,
shell-game victims. Left Stan my toaster, shelves,
a wire bird-cage, and, for once, nothing to say.
Except to ask if he could touch her skull.

Even now it makes no sense. Her precedents
I knew lurched out of focus: photos from France
after the Vichy fell, Jeannes and Sylvianes
who'd made Nazi moll; those Belfast girls

last-ditched by soldier boys or peelers; two-
toned Bergen-Belsen, bald sister to Fort Santiago.
Then Squeaky Fromm, the other Manson moms,
at Charlie's trial. Extremes of Joan of Arc,

or even Buddhist nuns. Hated, chastened—
or chaste, at least. Not what you'd run (I ran)
your fingers satisfied across, the stubble
surprising, soft as mink or fox, and arch

your back, as I did once she found me uptown,
say yes I give again when she went down—
and faster now, quick as the television
dropped after dishes to the curb—or slipped

gradually up, the seconds separating
as slowly as but more exquisitely than
ticks off expensive fifty-minute hours—
and some community service—all gone, and just

as easily forgotten the raft of former friends
I'd cursed and floated off the island. Shaved head,
her slender neck, dark shoulders—that was half—
or less—her most convincing argument.

## Pan in Arkansas

He's back again: bare chest and leather jacket,
his hair matted with mud and maple leaves,
a gash above his stubbled cheek, loose teeth,
one eye sealed up, the other blinking hard.
He's come from a beating behind the Baptist church,
some redneck groomsmen jumped him, got him with sticks,
tire irons, a knife. I take his silver Zippo,
Marlboro reds, and light us each a smoke.

    I made these pipes for music, not for clubbing
    hypocrites' heads. Look here—their hair and blood
    have blocked my reed, and my lips are chafed and split.
    Christ, John. Don't they know I was there at Cana,
    beside the Fish, his next of kin—his twin,
    filling those jars of wine above the brim?

# My House and the House Next Door

In the overgrown lot next door, backhoes
have turned up an infant graveyard. The stones
are rotting under orange lichen, sunk hip-deep

in mud. One's toppled over, trapping
a health-club flyer, condom wrapper, rain pooled
in the grooves of its brief inscription. Last night

the young woman from the stone cottage
on my other side slipped after a year sober
and passed out in the grass. I'm sure

she's heard the fighting in the bedroom,
door panels cracking, the good-byes, the late
long-distance phone calls. And one mad night,

crackling light from a fire on the stoop
as I burned my ex's paintings. The freight train
comes, metal thumping wood, a relief.

It silences our apologies. How have I
arrived here, my house anchored to the middle
of the country, moored between peaks

in the Ozarks' eroded plateau? The machines
have plowed around a sunflower nine feet tall.
It nods over the foundation of a long-gone

house, storm cellar built before the war.
My neighbor and I walk together looking
at the tiny stones. There's nothing, we agree,

we want more in this world than children.

# Bachelorhood

Argument—hostile sex—burgeoning dread:
Phoebe said, Box me at Connacht's Irish bar
again, love. But all my brilliant crack was feldspar,
her hillside's silver eucalyptus dead.
I dated slim Persephone instead.
Anti-depressants warmed our winter star;
in the mailroom, someone else's unlocked car,
wherever we might get caught, she made our bed.

Too bad I felt confined by public space
despite her kinky talk, black net and lace,
and Zoloft's little death anticipates
those ashes greater than the greatest lust:
Persephone can never forget we're dust,
separate. I spent some time a celibate.

II

# In the Kills

And the LORD said to Satan, Behold, he is in your hand.

*The Book of Job* (6: 2)

## I. Comforter to Job

Silt the kills with creek-bed sand
when morning branches from tree of heaven

Catch crab apples floating tidal wash
cordgrass cattail and the common reed

Vault trolley car cables flattened barges
gray caboose with rusted couplings

Start shorebirds from their hidden nests
or wind-cropped birch and stunted locust

Dry cattail punks on rotting docks
the tarpaper roofs of pilot shacks

Span bars and flats and brackish streams
the spits and shoals and marshwort strands

Pass oil tank farms and leaning beams
kill-bottoms dredged for sunken cars

Cross railroad yards where flatbeds haul
median blocks bulkhead slabs and loader cranes

Scale caving roofs of gutted mills
the paint factory's empty window frames

Stand evenings under broken skylights
where elder bends and spike grass grows

## II. An Audience

Pick up a rifle—wrist-rocket—or just a rock—
for God's sake, knock me down mid-air. These kills
are filled and bilked. I've flown over the smoke

like kingfisher come for morning offerings,
more flights from Newark, tower lights, and lights
which blink in answer on the airplane's wings,

and ringing the city's throat, or girding its waist—
its gilded waste—a whole necklace of lights,
a belt of tiny bird hearts, in turn replaced

by one rude stone, the sun rising through mist
behind the harbor. There's no relief in drink.
Drag me through cattail punks, tie my wrists

to gun racks, ankles to pick-up bumpers and quarter
me—lay me down in landfill, marshwort take
me under, weigh me down while suckers plunder

flesh from my arms and legs, nibble my toes—
just toss the undertow whatever's left.
And where I come to rest, let thistles grow

instead of barley, cockle instead of grass.
He sees my ways and counts my steps—He gives
no answer—though it's all I've ever asked.

III. Answer to Job

Have you kept watch beyond the skyline of blue fires
rippling from steel towers, squat brick chimneys
belching jetties of yellow smoke, the networks
of PVC pipe and signal lights, train tracks
and bridges, tug-boat docks and loading cranes?

Have you conjured kelp from the rivermouth, steelheads
to swim the canal's still water, turtles to amble over car doors
and batteries? Have you towed horseshoe crabs in your wake,
the silvering over at evening, grey-backed wingspan of herons
landing, low-tide along the marshwort strand, rose-lit and blinking?

Where were you when I carted sleep through the kills?
When I rode horseback, did you canter up the river path
and circle the refinery? Have you shied at the lights
of chimney fires, reared up and been bridled? Can you
wake men when they're strapped to your back like saddles?

Do you rust girders of Leviathan plants with rain you
drive from the sky, tide you draw up past sinking barges?
Who can stand before me? And who will wade the kills to jimmy
factory doors, start old assembly lines, who fix gutted
walls, caving roofs, when everything under the sky is mine?

IV. Settling Up

I'll wear self-loathing like sacking sewn from weeds.
I'll cake my face with mud, the foulest grit,
killbottom silt. The road I'll hitch exceeds
the Turnpike's reach. I'll cross Route One and slit
some dragon's throat, blood-soak the old stone paving
on Saint George Avenue. Crows will circle, raving.


Wait. Highways, billboards and oil drums, the raw
lamplight around refineries, the distillery
with towers flaming, lovely, deadly—you see
(though beautiful at night) they're less than straw.

Brooks, rivers, creeks wash inland seas with silt
and chem-plant seep. But I am a tide which fills
the empty spaces. I spread beyond the kills;
I come like water, restoring where you've built.

# III

# New Corinthian: Letter to Paul

My love like love of love petitions deconstruction
My love is fire's form, flames beyond its function

Government of my love would shame the left-wing fascist
Love to my love is like the jock strap to Priapus

My love is ugly and dignified after Eleanor Roosevelt
My love says nothing and insists its silences are heartfelt

My love mimes Sydney Carton, selfless and misanthropic
My love's Gospel is by Thomas, incendiary, gnostic

My love is the Minotaur reflected in the bulls-eye
My love is to dust what singing is to pigsty

The hospital of my love is sealed against infection
The language of my love can not bear inflection

My love is nihilism choked with a trombone
My love is a cat sucking marrow from a ham bone

My love is spent like wind through the lupines
My love is over there, saluting from the margins

# Newark Underworld

He hurtles out of the pink-rimmed darkness
on one repeated note: B-sharp, drops off
with a splash among the iron fish

funking up the canal. The notes creep away
like vines strangling the feet of refineries,
binding ankles, knocking knees. A measured stop

to inhale the smoke stumbling low-waisted,
eaten with rickets, from factory chimneys
before he blows open bar doors down Vailsburg.

The Blarney's all gone, except shamrock shapes
on mats in the urinals, green bow-ties and tinsel
glued to the ceiling. Dust blocks the windows

of apartments overhead. The tenor's silent.
But the whole room spins with pink and yellow lights,
sirens and strobes, smoke smelling of cherries

and engine cleaner. The music's industrial,
metronomic. Silver curtains spread and women
come out dancing, stripped already. It's hard

to tell which one she is—so many thin brown limbs
moving at once, the light too bright and cut
with darkness, the music dragging at his feet.

It's guesswork, but he grabs one by the boot, hauls
her off over his shoulder before the bouncer's
even seen him. He's not spun around, he won't

look back. He can feel the bones of her shin
through the leather, her fists on his shoulder.
He's hidden in smoke, masked by mud

from the river bottom—of course she doesn't
know him, she can't, and though her red hair
is shorter, cut curiously straight, she's his.

# Dreaming of Feet

*Cold feet augur a disappointment in love*

I was eating moths' wings and magnolia leaves,
white lipstick, blond hair, and purple nails,
tampax wrapped in tissue, ash on marmite toast.
You can imagine how many pints of beer
it took to get that voodoo grub down.


*Aching feet mean family problems*

Your mother taught you to prepare leg of man:
baste it with soy sauce and honey,
stuff it with rice, onion, and rosemary,
and roast it over low heat for three days.
Cook it outdoors, is what she suggested,
because man's meat has a gamey smell.


*Loss of feet indicates unexpected obstacles*

Homesick you marched three Mayan glyphs in snow:
Sky Penis, the Jaguar, and Coatlicue
with her crown of skulls, necklace of hands.
When you climbed a tree to see your footprints
you shook loose a great cloud of crows.
They came hooking south along the coast to me,
skimming and hawking, chasing away seagulls—
now she's alone, and now she's not, act quickly—
but, you know, the whole murder was too late.


*Burning feet represent jealousy*

The palmist at Spring Fest opened your hand,
bent back your pinkie, and drew us a picture

of your two future sons. Everyone laughed
when your newest boyfriend kindled his hands.
At the air rifle range I missed the paper stars.
The woman I was with reached for a stuffed rabbit,
but I had shot out its pink plastic eyes.


*Bare feet suggest new sexual experience*

Iceland's sole export that year was a vampire
obsessed with Lord Byron. While he did nothing
for the economy, he did get us drunk
and started us dancing. I kissed you finally,
during some deep merengue. Soon everyone
was kissing. What a crowd of lips and feet.
I was reaching for your boots when your man arrived,
but his timing was off. He didn't dance slow enough.


*Pain from sore feet forecasts comfort in old age*

Put your hands in my hair, wipe the moth dust
and magnolia leaves away from my mouth,
press my face to the crown of heads,
the necklace of hands, tattooed across your belly.
I'm listening here, just pausing a minute,
before making my way down to your feet.

# Winter Garden

The long hike back after dinner and drinks.
A first date, so the foyer's the measure. Once
again our recent exes—hers to a lemon grove
just south of San Jose, mine a little wisp

of smoke along the Mersey, Thames, or Liffey.
I suppose there's punishment in unfinished stairs,
exposed pipes and wires. But look, her whole
house hatches winter witchcraft: flowers crowd

tables and windowsills, tulips and lilies
in painted pots, cut crocus, iris, and primrose,
honeysuckle and pomegranate hung in baskets
on the landing, a bowl of poppies beside the bed.

Talk takes us easily over expert hedge rows,
mines neglected root cellars, all those bulbs
in underground storage. She bends to punch pillows
and comforter, suspending dust like pollen.

## The Polish Question

The rain that falls tonight on Merck's
brick chimneys, Exxon's clear blue flames,
dirt causeways to the public works,
the slackened jaws of loading cranes,

slick hiss of tires on the Turnpike,
a road crew's sparking hammer blast,
the pause, pop, cut-out scud a bike
makes stopping at an overpass,

stark quiet near the exit ramp
where commuters slow to rubber-neck
a jack-knifed truck and ambulance,
the flares that mark an earlier wreck

and roadside furrows tow-trucks left—
are nowhere on our map of scars
and birthmarks—but possibly suggest
our bedroom lit by passing cars.

# The Raft of the Medusa

## I.

We weren't satisfied with the thermometer
in a glass on the bedside dresser, moon charts
and temperature ledger in the drawer below.
We set the radio alarm to a cowpoke station
from Waco, your mother swallowed garlic pills
and I chewed ginger root each morning, while each night
we anointed each other behind the ears and knees
and in several more sensitive spots with pinkish paste
that smelled of sardines and stung the skin—with no
*manghuhula* we had to make do with a recipe
we'd pinched from a book on the sorcerers of Cebu.

The sun shone through the Water-Bearer's beakers,
and all weekend long the moon hid in the crook
of the Scorpion's tail. We took to our bed
with honey and biscuits, dried apricots and mangoes,
a mist of lavender mint. The butterfly blooms
of orchids and rosehips fluttered in the drafts
about the windowsills; we plucked them from
the air and crushed them in our palms,
massaged them into wrists and shoulders. Two
long days and nights we spent like that, the bed
become a raft far from the shores of telephone
or television, front door and mailbox, a raft
floating you into the world, your bulrush basket.

II.

Beyond the harpies of childhood, your family tree
with roots on four continents, a half-dozen islands,
what cruelties have we conjured you here to face?
Our bed with sagging box spring and broken slats,
the metal frame a hazard to naked shins,
it was no *Raft of the Medusa*, but I know
a day may come when you'll believe it was:
the journey to the colony cut short,
the soldiers mutiny, captain severs ropes,
a hundred and fifty drift for fifteen days,
a tenth survive by sacrificing the weak
and eating the dead until the *Argus* arrives.

When tempted by the easy analogy
remember your mother's point: Géricault chose
his scene from many, some more, some less grisly—
the teasing white butterfly, the cutting up
of shipmates' flanks, the riots come with twilight—
and still he couldn't keep his painting free
from platitudes contesting hope and despair.
The foreground harbors its grizzled *père*, the dead
surround him, sprawled across his thigh (his son?)
a young man's naked corpse, so rescue makes
no difference now, and after all, the men
expecting the ship to save them, that spot
on the horizon, are, we know, mistaken.

III.

Géricault makes his own mistake as well:
most of his models were healthy men. (His friend
Delacroix's there, such lovely shoulders, his arm,
the fulcrum, reaches for the sea.) Though others
he painted he purchased from the morgue—
the half-gnawed hand, the open-eyed, severed heads,
the blue-veined, articulately-muscled legs—
even they aren't foul enough. Lay waste
those limbs with salt and sun, two weeks of hunger,
a stranger diet, and you'll come closer to
the truer truth. But never mind, *anak*.

You'll learn the more important things, in art
and life; Géricault's raft, our raft, though both
inaccurate, will do. The hope we have
for you seems simple, even sad, in its lack
of magnitude, but I'll consider us all blessed
if you can laugh at either *Raft of the Medusa*,
and a little harder at the worms that spin
invisible ropes to tie them to each other.

# Perpetuum Carmen
### Gabriel

Already one of us, you spend your day
in conversation with yourself. You sew
ecstatic arias to recitativo,
stark catalogues of basest hunger for change

in tenor, contralto, basso, soprano, stray
staccato syllables of consonant
stutter and morphing vowel. Revenant
in E, you batter monolithic A

until it crumbles into Ums and O's.
You grow contemplative and growl again—
you're at the parapet, the echo's plain,
too late to stop the fall. Your singing slows,

accommodates two fingers, fist, the strain
of gum and jaw on wrist. It's first and last,
the humming comes through skin and cycles fast,
it cuts the cutting teeth, descant to pain.

# Urban and His Daughter

Do not touch my mouth, for I wish to make
a pure offering to the Celestial God.
                    Saint Christine of Tyre

Urban's uncertain how her lover will come—
Shower of gold, white bull or satyr, field
Of fires igniting like poppies in morning sun.

Her tower is made of marble quarried above
Parma, a lure for Jove. She swallows stones,
Lets blood in secret, anticipates the dove.

In sleep she speaks with Agatha and Agnes,
Wakes to the shadow of wooden wheels, a love
Made manifest in shattered bones, the wagons

That carry thieves and heretics to the rack.
She promises to pray; Urban makes plans
For a child with Helen's hair or Heracles' back.

*

An angel bearing bread and lamb arrives
To end her fast, encourages her to break
Her father's gold and silver idols. The wives

Of Christians begging at the tower's base
Gather the shards that shower down. Their lives
Are spared by a miracle: he sees the face

Anticipated become a swarm of gold
And silver bees the beggars net with lace.
His urns of fat and incense bowls grow cold.

*

The wheel's the first of many punishments,
Fire built below, oil poured above. He folds
Her limbs in heated irons, flays her open

With whip and blade. She's bitten by snakes, her breasts
Are torn off and tongue ripped out, before the men
In Urban's service desert him. His god rests

On a frozen mountain top. His daughter's throat
Is healed by heretic psalms, and in the west
The sun is cut in quarters. He watches boats

Returning from Crete and Sicily catch fire
On the horizon, cargoes of ash and dust.
How like his daughter's god—demanding lust
Be burned inside, a cold fire, yielding no child.

# Vengeance

How qualify love for a God who'd wager
with Satan, prop Job—childless, penniless,
riddled with boils he scraped with potsherds, salved
with ash—between them? Who stranded Ruth to numb
her fingers barley-gleaning among strangers?
Whose nightingale trill stumped Abraham, put Isaac
on the block at knife-tip? Fear, respect,
due any desert patriarch, come easily.

But think how sweetly I loved my father when
he saved me in the alley from Dog-Star Freddy,
his troop of runners, sadistic thugs who'd just
as soon grope as punch you, drag you to the basement,
for once not letting me fight my own fight, Dad's
fists coming down like waves on Egyptian cavalry.

# How the Dog-Star Got His Name

Some said he was born beneath the hottest star,
but don't believe it—his mother dropped him howling,
his foal-legs hobbled, cleft palate whistling up
January's goat, the star-climber Capricorn.

Or else it was the way he bent us boys
and girls over cinder-block stacks, the arms
of his uncle's easy-chair down the moldy basement.
And later they said he played bitch in prison,

humming growl, sweat burning his eyes, free condoms
clenched between teeth. They said, remember how
he dressed in drag come Halloween? A crew
of blood-stained cheerleaders, Charlie's Angels,

saber-toothed cat-women in spandex pants—
he wore the same yellow wig every year, gummed
plastic fangs under his own botched hare-lip.
But his name is older than all that, older than

the star tattoo he carved himself, six-pointed
collar around a black-eyed dog, which came
near killing him with tetanus. He was no
dog-bite survivor, star-baiting rock or mensch,

just victim of an unsteady hand, his spray-can.
The morning my buddy Paul caught him tagging
the walls at Saint Mary's, a simple asterisk,
stick-figure pig, was all the mural he could make.

Paul served at mass without a word; that night
we fixed his sketch with half my gear, whole cans
of Apollonian Gold, transformed his pig
with heavy-lidded sun, a canine snout.

The face was Freddy's, beatified. Dog-Star,
I signed it. I gave him his name. They said
the little kids looked up to him, called him
the night-time sun, the summer star, but how

we hated him. It took all six altar boys
with steel-wool brushes, buckets of turpentine,
a hose snaking across the parking lot
from the rectory garden, to scrub him away.

# Free Union

*After Breton*

My wife whose hair is an ocean-crossing in winter
Whose thoughts are a crow's flight
Whose temples are the seeds of thunder
And the echo of pearl
My wife whose mouth is a snakebite
Whose teeth are tombstones to ideas
Whose eyelids are songs carried hidden in the pocket
Whose eyebrows are a field of feeding martins
Whose neck is a forest fire

My wife whose ears are seahorses under the anemones
Whose shoulders are lightning in a snowstorm
Whose fingers are cypresses stepping from the lagoon
Whose fingers are starlings
My wife whose nails leave an imprint of cobblestone streets
Whose eyes are mine-shafts opening across a golf course
Whose breath is a swarm of fireflies
Whose hands are tea roses floating in an ice chest
My wife whose hips are suggestions of wisteria
And the memory of water summoned by divining rod

My wife whose breasts are islands choked with bougainvillea
Whose wrists are bottle-rockets sparklers Roman candles
Whose arms are highways singing the Tennessee mountains
Whose back is a school of dolphins sewing up the Gulf Stream
Whose waist is a coral snake curled up in the milk jug
Whose feet saddle the backs of sparrows
Whose legs are evening primrose

My wife whose thighs are carp idling beneath a bridge
Whose calves are votive candles
Whose ankles are cocoons summoning their silkworms
My wife whose eyes are cups of anise
Whose eyes are rainfall on the heather

Whose eyes are the sleep that comes with fever
And the dreams of bearded iris
My wife with the eyes that are a cloudburst
A cliff-dive a border-crossing
Tugboats chuffing around the inlet
Sunlight in the sea from which I never surface

# Nicholas, Flying

*Plum Island, Mass.*

Our two-year-old is flying around the house
again, dipping from television corner
to kitchen table, soaring over hardwood floors

in salt-collared boots, pinning tight turns around
obstacles—slippers shaped like tigers, Tarzan
and Power Ranger wrestled to a draw,

the setter barking at his feet. We can't
help laughing, how smoothly he flies, how gracefully
he lowers, doubled at the waist, expands

arms out, his fingers flying creatures of their own,
his hair still sun-streaked half a dozen shades
from brown to platinum flung in a startling arc,

the curve of neck and back like something equally
at home in air or sea. The currents he soars are arias
of loss I can't bear hearing since his birth,

Puccini's *Suor Angelica*, bad days even *Tosca*,
although he flies when we play them. (See, at least,
I've saved him the saddle of too much beauty, the span

of forehead hauled from Sicily, the hooked
nose, median of a wide, East-Asian divide
between his Murphy's eyes.) Nicholas, we call,

how will you land? I'll just fly, he says, taking
his cues from God knows what—the herons gone,
kingfishers flown, hawks hunting up the salt marsh

and hills behind, a lone crow standing over skunk
or cat, some frozen stump of road kill—one day
he started flying, like nothing we had taught him.

# Why Not Dig Up the Dog?

> I see by your eagerness...that you expect to be informed
> of the secret with which I am acquainted; that can not be.
> Mary Shelley, *Frankenstein*

Why not dig up the dog? What parent's not
part hypocrite? To wit, he's bone and leather,
a Giacometti we can't make animate
with plug and socket, son. He's dead forever.

I'd be a monster not to sweeten it some:
Let old bones fertilize; our setter flies
with angels—that's not him, that stick of dumb
brown calcium. Of course I sympathize,

although by now our dog's more dogwood bloom,
a calla lily. The rest is heresy,
and hard to undo—that *soul*'s an empty room
or shorthand for a jolt of electricity.

# My Father's House

From Red Hook, Brooklyn, to Bergenline Ave.,
near Merck's in Rahway to Seaside Heights,
my father moves to places where
it's never dark, never quiet. His sleep
spreads under dock lights and barges,
the red brick fires of factory chimneys
and Exxon's silver, flame-hipped towers.
Summers he's hop-scotched garage apartments,
studio lofts and rented rooms, then wintered
off-season in beach-strip motels. He craves
the boardwalk lamps and high-tide foam,
that perpetual low shore-break roar.
Out of work once I crashed with him,
a friend's unfinished condo—doors, trim,
and ceiling, stripped sheet-rock walls, everything
painted a mad-house white and pocked
with empty hooks. Parking lot lights
glossed the window shades all night,
and sweeping high-beams turned
uncurtained sliders to abalone gates.
Our fridge held only beer and condiments.
I've got it wrong if I sound ungrateful;
he gladly gave his bedroom for the couch.
Better, later, to bunk for weeks at a time
in his suite of rooms stacked behind
the old Sandpiper kitchen—quick dinners
of clams, grilled grouper or snapper, late
evenings of black-jack and poker, and always
the smell of mussels and steamers, melting
butter, broiled flounder, haddock or cod
frying in lard. Hard to be lonely there,
with the dishwasher's hiss and coffee grinding,
cooks shouting, laughing, slapping down
the shoulder-snap ring of the expediter's bell,
and early mornings, the rodents scratching.

> But now—

he's never lived anywhere quite like this—
no docks, no sidewalks here, and just one streetlight.
He swims transmogrified, a tropical fish,
through the subdued blues of giant-screen
TV, or velvety aqua and paler-green
computer glow, in this sub-division split-
level, his girlfriend's kit. Her place
is packed with things, a cache of knick-knacks
fired from Swiss ceramics, Delft and glass
or molded plastic, the chicks just hatching,
bears clapping, ham-cheeked school-kids dancing.
Stuffed animals hog couches, walls are quilts
of needle-point and calendars, and Dad's room
is dimmed by hand-sewn curtains—never mind
the home-made dolls stitched from linen,
pottery frogs, the skunk that chirps
and lifts its tail when an intruder passes.
Who knows what's stopped him here, some odd
new happiness, a lease's absence,
inertia's advances, but there he sleeps—
his silver hair grown almost dark again—
and takes his phone calls, late ones, at least.

# Two Ogres

*explaining the New War to my son, 2002*

Here's Polyphemus, still drunk and half-asleep,
with clumps of human hair, flecks of skin
matted in bloody stubble on his chin,
his single eye branded by the wily Greek
whose name is Nobody. Beyond his reach
and raving—makeshift patch devised from one
cramped hand, the other beating dust—Anon
and friends escape, strapped to the bellies of sheep.

Or else it's Kong, cradling platinum-
crowned queen in palm (here's one that he won't eat),
striking at buzzing planes, the distracting light
from skyscrapers and radio towers, and some
unlucky janitor, who sees too late
the hairy hand, mashed nose, red eyes, aping flight.

# Hyon Gok Sunim

*(The Paper Boys)*

I've cursed his shaven head, and I'd begrudge him
the crust of bread, clump of rice in his begging bowl,
but I must have loved him once—nothing short
could have called me from bed before the sun broke

over Merck's brick chimneys, and every week I woke
beneath the pink dome of Saturday night, burning tops
of Esso's silver towers framed by bedroom window,
floor lit from flame to flame, the neon bottle

on the distillery billboard blinking still,
infinitely full and pouring. Those early Sundays
we collected Curtis from the Riverside Arms,
his afro enormous, sleep-crushed, a dented globe,

and rode the station-wagon tailgate three across,
shuddering over train tracks and bridges, transmission
wired by a twisted pin, muffler scraping up sparks
below our feet, wheel-wells and half-dozen seats

heaped with newsprint. That future-monk's mad father,
a spoiled priest, failed football coach, moonlighting
night-watchman, hauled us up the hills into Watchung
and let us loose on the constipated lawns of the New

Chosen—descendants of the David of Winthrop, Bradford
and Mather—his voice a heated gust blasting us from house
to gabled house, admonishing us to pluck the worm, mind
the sunrise, marble fountains, City skyline, praise God

and move our F-ing asses, till our arms ached
and palms and t-shirts clearly bore the headlines
(Cambodian Fix, Dick Nixon's Tricks, Mets and A's
Make It Seven, the breathless puns on Saigon, Kompong

Som, yet another subway bomb). And for what in return?
A more comfortable seat, Dunkin Donuts on the way home,
the occasional dollar, and the promise, from father
and ten-year-old son, that we were building character.

\*

As if character were collateral to bank and trade on,
and every Sunday we hoisted ourselves a bit closer
to creatures we've become: so Curtis incubated
Raheem, while Paul invented Hyon Gok Sunim. Even I,

though unconverted, have multiplied, lied, cozied up
to the dozen nicknames of creation, sent my son
and smaller siblings out rowing through chum, knelt
and sacrificed to a whole slew of gods, most false,

some still passing for true, and thank God for family,
the ability to generate your own company, or I'd be
lonely, with Curtis gone silent, separatist, suffocated
under braided Muslim robes and razor, and the tiny fire

that was Paul extinguished on a Korean mountain-top.
His new epistles make their way from the monastery,
not as prompt as the Sunday paper, nor as thick, but
just as fattened with satisfaction, pious flatulence.

Ego as Scapegoat, War on Desire, Death-Love, Dukkha,
Chastity, and Congratulations, *fatherhood's deprivations*
*must have snuffed your flame of self, welcome the end*
*of illusion...* But I've only hidden my light behind

a bushel, or else he'd see even from the monastery
the humming pink curve of the night-time sky, desire
brighter than Exxon's refining lights, Gordon's liquid
glow, gin bottle tipped and pouring brilliant fire,

clouds chugging from Merck's brick chimneys, engines
of yellow envy sculling the sky, and my picnic
below, the checkered blanket, basket of chicken
for Sloth and Gluttony: to prove him wrong I'd become

a figure from the old morality plays, fattened, bald,
mirror-waving, bent on self-destruction, mouth stuffed
with fingers, genitals, horseflesh, an offering of skin
and fatty thighbone; oh, yes, it must have been love.

# My Son's Lost Languages

Words hide from his Lola in places she'd
forgotten, crown like shoots nursed only
in shade: a garden of albino narcissus,
overturned rock, the watering can caked with rust.
When she closes her eyes, beach umbrellas open,
heartbreak's waterfall rolls from her shoulders,
verbs for marathon swimming, frustrating
unbuttoning, snap their tails across her tongue.

His greatest grandfather's an aging superman
with faith like a lightning rod held up
to sunshine. They've bulldozed all his phone booths,
but he's learned how to cross his own wires,
extracting Charlie from Calogero
despite the gob full of dentures. We take Kay
for Carmella, catch enough to pass coffee
and biscuits, turn the lights off when we leave.

But who will be *his* friend Dennis Rivera, translating
a summons, tap-dancing shut-offs, turning "F"
to "Fantastic" on his brother's report card?
Who will teach impudence like Chetti Martinetti,
whose grandmother spun her weeds from foreign curses,
stirred Friday's bean soup, animated as stone?
Who knows where he'll find a mouthful of turf-smoke,
which words he'll bury in coal-dusted basements?

# Calling

He crosses slag heaps behind the laundry, new
Neolithic, face hidden by mud and hair,
one dirty denim shirt-sleeve gone, signaling arm
bruised, covered with welts or sarcoma. What am I
doing back here in mail-order flannels, leather-soled
shoes? I can't name the impulse that took me off
the train to the city, but this is no dream. He holds up
the shell of a cell-phone plucked from the river
and asks if I'll buy it. Anything can happen.

I'll lead with my left, aim to split the skin
below his eye-socket with my wedding ring.
Or I can scrabble over a stack of pallets,
head for the alley, shortcut to our old street.

He waves the phone so it catches the sun.
It's silver, clean from the river—for a second
I'm blind—but he forces it into my hand. From where
we're standing we can just see the rusted dome
of Rahway Prison. Last I heard, Freddy was there
or buried under it. Sure, I'll call *him*.

Or Curtis, who nearly bled to death from hit-
and-run while crazy Frieda sat and watched.
Or Ball who broke my nose once, heart twice.
Or smart-ass Bumpy who left for MIT
and stirs the Persian Gulf in a nuclear sub.
Or Paul whose scrip—perverse black bag—hauled East
to east, beyond stark Golgotha's squared-off teeth,
to some fermented eagle's nest hung above Seoul.
Or silent Keesha who thanked me for *Gateless Gate*—
I thought the book would make her moderate.

The salesman's gone already, disappeared
down river with the rest, past muddy clumps
of skunk cabbage, pigweed, spiderwort,
a gutted pickup chassis, still holding my change.

John Hennessy grew up in New Jersey and went to Princeton on a Cane Scholarship. He has lived in New York, Amsterdam, and Austin, and completed graduate degrees at the University of Texas and the University of Arkansas. His poems appear in *The New Republic*, *The Yale Review*, *New Letters*, *Ontario Review*, *Fulcrum Annual*, *Harvard Review*, *Salt* (UK), *Notre Dame Review*, *Jacket* (Australia), *The Sewanee Review*, and *Best New Poets 2005*. In the fall of 2007 he will be the Resident Fellow at the Amy Clampitt House; these days he lives with his family in Amherst and teaches at the University of Massachusetts.

Printed in the United States
70832LV00008B/82-105